COLUMBUS
AND THE
AGE OF
EXPLORATION

Stewart Ross

Illustrations by Ken Stott

The Bookwright Press
New York · 1985

LIFE AND TIMES

Julius Caesar and the Romans
Alfred the Great and the Saxons
Canute and the Vikings
William the Conqueror and the Normans
Richard the Lionheart and the Crusades
Columbus and the Age of Exploration
Elizabeth I and Tudor England

Further titles are in preparation

First published in the United States in 1985 by
The Bookwright Press
387 Park Avenue South
New York, NY 10016

First published in 1985 by
Wayland (Publishers) Ltd
49 Lansdowne Place, Hove
East Sussex BN3 1HF, England

ISBN 0 531 18012 3
Library of Congress Catalog Card Number: 84-73568

Printed by G. Canale & C.S.p.A., Turin, Italy

Contents

1 THE STORY OF COLUMBUS

Above *The caravel in which Columbus sailed to the New World in 1492.*

Land ahoy!

In the crow's nest the lookout screwed up his eyes against the glare of the tropical sun. Beneath him the little 40-ton ship *Nina* rolled heavily in the Atlantic swell. The sailor took a piece of dry biscuit from his pocket. It tasted foul, but there was no other food. They had been at sea for forty days now and supplies were getting perilously low.

Looking behind him, the man on watch could see the *Santa Maria*, Christopher Columbus's ship, and a smaller vessel, the *Pinta*. There was nothing else but the broad blue sea.

Over the last few days Columbus had found it difficult to persuade his men to continue their westward voyage. The crews, many recruited from Spanish jails and slums, muttered of mutiny. There was no way to China, they said. They wanted to return home before Columbus's crazy ideas killed them all. But Columbus would not listen.

Once more the lookout turned his attention to the sea in front of him. His eyes ached and his tongue was dry with thirst. Suddenly he shouted, pointing frantically to the sea ahead of the *Nina*. Bobbing up and down in the water was a branch with berries on it. This was a sure sign that they were near land.

At two o'clock that night, Friday October 12th, 1492, a sailor on board the *Nina* sighted the coast. The crew of the three ships went wild with delight: they had made it! So Columbus had been correct. They had reached China by sailing to the west. How wrong they were!

Below *In the early hours of Friday October 12, 1492, a sailor on lookout in the crow's nest of the* Nina *sighted land for the first time in 40 days. Columbus, who led the expedition, believed he had discovered China. In fact, he had reached the Bahamas in the Caribbean Sea.*

A man with a dream

Christopher Columbus was born in Genoa in 1451. He first went to sea at the age of fourteen and by the time he was thirty he knew the Atlantic from Iceland to Ghana. He had learned to make maps and charts, had been shipwrecked and had even fought with pirates! All this time, however, one idea was growing in his mind: to discover a new route to the rich lands of the Far East.

Columbus knew of China and Japan from travelers' tales and from Greek writings. Also he was an ambitious man who wanted for himself the wealth and glory that would come to the first European who could find an easy way to the East.

Most men in Columbus's day knew that the world was round, but they believed it to be much smaller than it is. Columbus thought Japan was only about 4,800 km (3,000 miles) west of Spain, when really it is about 19,200 km (12,000 miles). Also, the existence of North and South America was unknown. So Columbus though he could sail west from Europe to China in a few weeks. You can get a good idea of Columbus's view of the world from the World Map of Henricius Martellus which was printed in 1489 (see page 10).

During the 1480s Columbus tried to find someone willing to pay for his voyages of exploration. He approached the rulers of Spain, Portugal, France and England, but they all refused. Almost in despair, he again turned to King Ferdinand and Queen Isabella of Spain. This time they agreed to help.

Thus it was that Admiral Christopher Columbus set sail in 1492 with three ships and eighty-eight men, carrying with him a letter of introduction to the emperor of China. Just under six weeks later his ships reached the Bahamas in the Caribbean Sea. Although he didn't realize it, Columbus had discovered a new continent.

Later voyages

Below *Columbus captured some of the native "Indians" who lived on the Caribbean islands and transported them back to Spain to show to King Ferdinand and Queen Isabella.*

Columbus returned to Spain in 1493. Ferdinand and Isabella were at Barcelona, and the new hero entered the city in triumph, bearing gifts of gold, cotton, mysterious plants and strange birds for his patrons. He also brought back natives from the islands he had discovered. These unfortunate captives he called "Indians" because he thought they came from India.

The highest honors were given to Columbus and later that year he was equipped with three galleons and fourteen smaller ships for another westward expedition (1493-94).

On his first voyage, Columbus had discovered several West Indies islands: the Bahamas, Cuba and Hispaniola, where he had left some men. When he returned he founded a larger settlement, which he called Isabella. He then proceeded to explore Cuba, believing it to be part of mainland China.

The strain of these voyages was enormous. Columbus had to navigate through unknown tropical seas, organize supplies and work with other greedy adventurers, who often did not take easily to his ruthless command. At one time he lay sick in Isabella for five months. On another occasion, on his third voyage (1498), the jealous rival explorer Bobadilla sent him back to Spain in chains.

We will never know whether Columbus realized that he had not reached the Far East. On his third voyage he discovered the South American mainland at Venezuela, while his last journey (1502-04) took him to Honduras and Nicaragua, which he mistook for Indo-China.

Exhausted by his travels, Columbus died in 1506. He was a hard master, and his treatment of the "Indian" natives was often disgraceful: many went back to Spain as slaves. Nevertheless Columbus deserves to be remembered as one of the greatest explorers of all time. After all, he had discovered a "New World."

Above *This fifteenth century woodcut shows Columbus bartering for gold with the local inhabitants, on his first voyage to Hispaniola.*

2 THE "OLD WORLD"

A small world

For the men and women of medieval Europe the world was small, isolated and unchanging. They believed that outside Christendom (the area inhabited by Christians) lay terrible natural and human dangers.

To the far north was the Frozen Zone of ice and snow, where it was too cold for anyone to live. To the south were the Muslim Moors of North Africa, ferocious pirates; beyond them was the Torrid Zone. Here it was said that the sea was so hot that it boiled. No one could

Below *This Ptolemaic map was drawn by the German cartographer, Henricius Martellus, in 1489.*

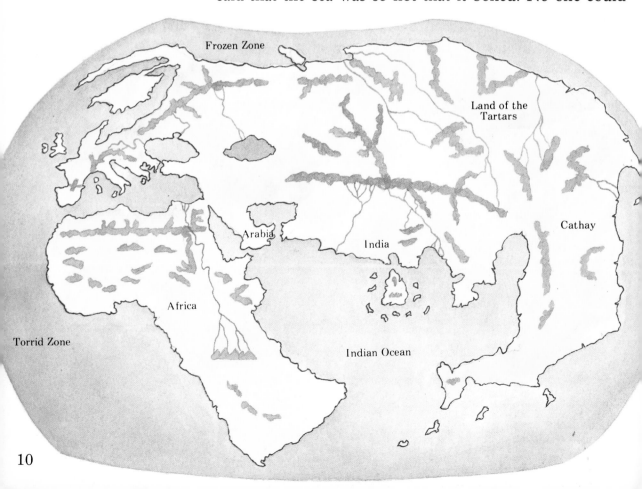

10

live here either. To the west rolled the impassable Green Sea of Darkness — the Atlantic. Finally, the fierce infidel empires of the Ottomans, Mamelukes and Mongols closed the eastern frontiers.

The vast majority of the inhabitants of Europe were peasants, who farmed very much as their ancestors had done for hundreds of years. Marriage, worship and other aspects of life changed hardly at all from one generation to another. Despite disturbances caused by plague, famine or war, village life went on as before, following the cycle of the seasons.

Inventions and discoveries were scarcely known. There was very little science: new ideas were considered dangerous and accepted only slowly. The powerful Christian Church taught that life on this earth was a painful but temporary trial: real life came after death.

With these attitudes, it is not surprising that before the fifteenth century, Europeans were reluctant to explore beyond the boundaries of their known world. Even had they wanted to, their ships were unsuitable, their navigation primitive, and travel by land slow and dangerous. So most of those who looked beyond Christendom did so with fear and in great ignorance.

Left A fifteenth century painting shows peasants plowing their land. This scene would have changed very little throughout the Middle Ages.

Broader horizons

Although it was isolated, medieval Europe was not totally cut off from the rest of the world. There was growing contact through trade, and geographical information could be found in stories and books. Medieval maps were hopelessly inaccurate, but by about 1400 more reliable ones were becoming available.

The writer Ptolemy had lived in Greece in the second century AD. Not only had he divided the world into 360 degrees of latitude and longitude, but he also drew reasonably accurate maps of Europe, Asia and Africa.

In the fifteenth century Ptolemy's ideas were spread by writers such as Sacrobosto, who argued strongly that the world was round, and Cardinal d'Ailly. Columbus's copy of d'Ailly's book *Imago Mundi*, with his comments in the margin, still exists today.

Below *Marco Polo, the Italian who explored vast areas of Asia in the last quarter of the thirteenth century, stayed for several years at the court of Kublai Khan, emperor of China. The court features as Xanadu in Samuel Coleridge's poem* Kubla Khan.

Also from ancient times came stories of Hanno the Phoenician who, in about 500 BC, sailed far down West Africa. In northern Europe sagas circulated about how Vikings, led by Leif Eriksson, had sailed the stormy North Atlantic west of Greenland to Vinland (or Wineland). In the eleventh century several Viking ships followed Leif to this fertile area but it is difficult to be sure that Vinland was in fact America.

About 250 years after the Vikings, the Italian family called Polo made equally exciting journeys, to the east. In 1271 Nicolo and his son Marco left Venice on 21 years of exploration. Traveling the overland trade routes of Asia to China, they reached Peking and the court of Emperor Kublai Khan. Marco recounted his amazing adventures in *The Description of the World*, in which he told of the wealth, power and civilization of the East. The book was widely read: Christopher Columbus had his own copy.

Above *Catalan merchants traveled far to seek the riches that came from trading with the East.*

3 WHY THEY WENT

Gold and spice

A Spanish adventurer, Bernal Diaz, said that he explored, "to serve God, to bring light to those who are in darkness." He then added with a smile, "and to grow rich!" Diaz had given the main reasons for European exploration: to spread Christianity, and to find wealth.

Some travelers, no better than pirates really, sought riches through plunder. Others dreamed of finding new fishing grounds. However, the most obvious wealth was land. Scores of men set out for the unknown, hoping to

Below *Gold was as precious in Columbus's time as it is now. Camel trains carried gold from Africa across the Sahara Desert, but it took a long time to reach Europe. Explorers hoped the source of the gold could be reached by sea more quickly.*

seize vast estates in foreign lands, where they could lead lives of leisure and never have to work again.

Trade was another source of wealth. Europe's most valuable business was with the East, which sent her ivory, jewels, silks and spices. Spice was essential for preserving food in the days before refrigeration and scientific farming. There wasn't sufficient food to keep animals alive over the long months when the grass didn't grow. Therefore, in the autumn, most stock had to be slaughtered and the meat preserved with salt and spice.

In the early fifteenth century, however, eastern trade was troubled. Anti-Christian Muslim empires cut many of the overland routes to Asia, such as that which Marco Polo had used. Merchants were forced to look for alternative ways to the East. The businessmen of Alexandria, in Egypt, who now handled most east-west trade, disliked the crude western goods they were offered. They wanted payment in gold.

Much of Europe's gold came across the Sahara Desert from West Africa. So Portuguese sailors sailed farther than they had ever done before down the west coast of Africa to find the source of this precious mineral. By 1500, 700 kilograms (1,500 lbs) of gold a year were reaching Lisbon in Portugal from the area we now call Ghana. No wonder the Portuguese called this the Gold Coast.

Above *The explorer, Marco Polo, opened up an overland trade route to Asia toward the end of the thirteenth century.*

In God's name

Bernal Diaz explored to serve God. We may find this strange, but it was the way people thought in his day.

Religion played a much greater part in people's lives then that it does today. Those who led voyages into the unknown were devout men, who wanted to convert the inhabitants of the lands they discovered to Christianity. The Portuguese marked where they had been on the west African coast with huge stone crosses: today we would probably use national flags.

Spain provided more overseas explorers than any other nation, but only in 1492 did the Spaniards finally reconquer southern Spain from the Muslims. Spanish soldiers were used to spreading their faith by the sword. The brilliant Cardinal Ximinez de Cisneros had given the Church in Spain a new lease of life in the early sixteenth century, so there were plenty of missionaries eager to travel with the explorers.

Sometimes the dreaded Spanish Inquisition would follow the missionaries to a country. The Inquisition had been established in Spain to punish heretics and encourage the conversion of Jews and Muslims to Christianity, and its methods could be very cruel. There were plenty of unbelievers for it to work on in the newly conquered lands.

In 1453 the Turks had captured Constantinople, one of the cornerstones of Christendom since Roman times. Its fall worried many Christians. By spreading their faith to new lands they felt that they were making up for losses in eastern Europe.

Religion and riches, however, were not the only reasons for exploration. There was at this time a new interest in Ancient Greece and Rome. As the Romans had done, men came to care a great deal for their reputations. Diaz boasted that he had fought in 119 battles — twice as many as Julius Caesar.

Above *Francis Ximinez de Cisneros, a sixteenth century Spanish cardinal, inspired many missionaries to spread the gospel overseas.*

Opposite *Torture was a common instrument of the Spanish Inquisition which tried to make sure that every Spaniard was a good Catholic, persecuting those who were not.*

4 A PASSAGE TO THE EAST

The adventurous Portuguese

The story of the Portuguese discoveries starts with a tall soldier, Prince Henry the Navigator (1394-1460). The prince devoted his life to the exploration of West Africa and the conversion of its inhabitants to Christianity. He established a secret base with a school of navigation at Sagres in southern Portugal — anyone taking a chart from there without permission was executed.

Henry sent out dozens of ships from Sagres, each captain urged to break through the "barrier of fear" that blocked the way south. By the time of Henry's death in 1460, Portuguese sailors had reached Sierra Leone. Ivory, gold dust and negro slaves were brought back to Sagres, but few Africans had accepted Christianity.

Below *Prince Henry the Navigator built a secret school of navigation at Sagres in southern Portugal. From there he planned expeditions by sea to explore the uncharted west coast of Africa.*

By 1474 the Portuguese had passed the swamps of the Niger delta and discovered that the African coast turned south again. Under a new royal patron, King John II, Diago Cao passed the mouth of the Congo River and reached the Tropic of Capricorn, 1,600 kms (1,000 miles) north of the Cape. Then, in 1487, Pedro de Covilhao left Portugal, disguised as a Muslim, and traveled for several years as far as India and East Africa. The vital information he smuggled back to Lisbon encouraged the sailors to continue their searches for a passage around Africa.

Bartholomeu Diaz also left Portugal in 1487. He journeyed far down the African coast with three ships to a base at 26 degrees south. Setting out against the contrary winds, Diaz finally turned east — and entered the Indian Ocean. His frightened men now forced him to return, but on the way back he first saw the southernmost point of Africa, which he called the Cape of Storms. Delighted at Diaz's success, however, John II renamed it the Cape of Good Hope, for a sea route to the east had finally been found.

Above *In 1488 Bartholomeu Diaz sailed around the Cape of Good Hope.*

Above *Henry the Navigator.*

In 1498, on his way to India, Vasco da Gama's ship, the San Gabriel, *bombarded the Arab trading port of Mombassa on the east coast of Africa.*

da Gama reaches India

Above *Vasco da Gama's flagship, the* San Gabriel.

Vasco da Gama was a wealthy courtier and diplomat, not a professional seaman. Yet his amazing return voyage to India (1497-99) was as great a feat as anything undertaken in the Age of Exploration. Columbus's return from his first voyage in 1493 caused much excitement. But the Pope declared most of the new land in the west to be Spanish, so the Portuguese were forced to continue to explore the east.

Vasco da Gama's expedition was carefully planned. He had four large and well-armed ships, weapons for all the 170 men, and manufactured articles for trading. Many of the crew were veterans. Finally, when all was checked and ready, the expedition set sail on July 8th, 1497.

Instead of hugging the coast, da Gama sailed southeast from Sierra Leone. For 96 days his ships did not sight land, the record for a European voyage at that time. However, the navigation had been so good that when they did see coast again they were almost at the Cape. By Christmas they were at Natal, and heading northeast. Farther up the East African coast they entered Sofala, a port mentioned by Covilhao. From here on the expedition was continually hampered by scurvy, and by Arab merchants who resented the European threat to their trade.

Vasco da Gama claimed that his mission was peaceful but he had weapons to defend himself and he even used torture to get information. So the Portuguese, partly trading, partly fighting, made their way up Africa and across the Indian Ocean to Calicut in India. The journey out had taken ten months. The return voyage was even tougher. At last, on September 9, 1499, having lost half his men, including his brother, and two ships, da Gama reached Lisbon again. He had sailed to India and back, succeeding where Columbus had failed.

Above *A portrait of Vasco da Gama.*

21

5 THE "NEW WORLD"

Vespucci and the South

On his last voyage, as he explored what is now Honduras, Columbus believed that he was only ten days sailing from the Ganges River in India. But other sailors were less confident of Columbus's geography — as early as 1494 men were writing of a "new world" in the west.

In 1499 the outline of South America began to emerge when Pinzon, one of Columbus's captains, sailed as far as the mouth of the mighty Amazon River. The next year, on another Portuguese voyage to India, Cabral discovered Brazil. If the continent that Columbus had reached was

Below *Explorers never knew what they might find in the lands they visited. They imagined South America to be full of cannibals and strange creatures. (Based on De Bry's impression of South America, drawn in 1596)*

indeed Asia, then the picture of it that was emerging was very different from Marco Polo's descriptions.

The man who finally proved Columbus wrong and gave his name to the new continent was Amerigo Vespucci (1454-1512). Vespucci was a well-educated Italian clerk, but also rather a shady character. In a famous book published in 1507 he claimed to have made four voyages. We can be sure of only two, however, in which he explored the American coast between Florida and the Plate River. He may even have ventured as far south as the Falkland Islands.

Above *A sixteenth century painting of the Italian explorer, Amerigo Vespucci.*

Amerigo Vespucci called the new continent America, "since Amerigo had found it." By 1520 it was quite clear that there was no way to the East through Central America. Sailors now faced a new challenge: to find a way around. They knew what they wanted to reach, for in 1513 the Spaniard Balboa had crossed the narrow neck of land that joins North and South America, and gazed on a vast new ocean. He called it the Pacific.

North America

Many Spanish sailors followed Columbus to the West Indies, all of them looking for a route to Asia. The hundreds of Caribbean islands and the coast of Central America took years to explore. But, by 1519, explorers had sailed right around the Gulf of Mexico and the unbroken nature of the central coastline was clear. Yet the North American shore was still relatively unexplored.

After the Vikings, the first European to sight North America was John Cabot (1450-98). In 1497 he claimed Newfoundland for his master King Henry VII of England, believing that he had landed on part of China. Two years later he disappeared while on a second voyage, but Corte Real, a Portuguese, continued the exploration before he too failed to return from an expedition.

The French completed the exploration of the North American coast. In 1524 King Francis I supported the expedition of Giovanni da Verrazano, an Italian, to find a northeastern passage to Asia. Verranzano sailed right up the coast, from Florida to Newfoundland, finding a magnificent harbor on the way. Today this "delightful place, situated among steep hills" is New York City, with the Verranzano Bridge spanning the Hudson River in memory of the first European to sail there.

By 1535 the Frenchman Cartier had explored the Canadian coast, and still no way through to Asia had been found in the north. Yet now the search was not quite so urgent. In 1522, thirteen years before Cartier's voyage, the greatest journey of all had been completed, a voyage around the world.

Above *An engraving of Sebastian Cabot, who explored the North American coastline with his father, John Cabot.*

Below *Shipwreck was a constant threat to sailors at this time. It can be assumed that John Cabot died in a shipwreck when he failed to return from an expedition in 1498.*

6 AROUND THE WORLD

The greatest voyage of all

Below In March 1521, Magellan led a raid on the island of Mactan in the Philippines. His small force of sixty Spaniards was overwhelmed by the natives and Magellan himself was hacked to death.

The Portuguese quickly realized the importance of da Gama's voyage to India. By 1518 regular cargoes of spices were entering Lisbon from the Moluccas, now part of Indonesia. The Spaniards had lost the race to Asia, but they were still determined to find a westerly passage there. Ferdinand Magellan finally achieved this for them.

Magellan was a Portuguese nobleman employed by the king of Spain. He was a skilled navigator, who had traveled widely and bore the scars of battles in North Africa and the East Indies. In 1519 his fleet of five ships, crewed by 237 men, left Spain with straightforward orders: sail west, and bring back spices from the Moluccas!

The ships sailed to Brazil and continued south for many months. Two captains were lost in mutinies and one ship was wrecked. Magellan was undaunted. In the autumn of 1520 three ships faced the worst weather in the world as they moved into the Pacific through the passage now called the Straits of Magellan. The fourth ship had fled home, carrying most of their supplies.

After the storms came starvation and disease as they plowed across the Pacific. The men were reduced to eating rats and leather. In March, Magellan was killed in a fight in the Philippines and Captain Elcano took command. Another ship was left behind because of a lack of crew. Finally, in November 1521, after a voyage of twenty-seven months, two vessels and 115 men reached the Moluccas.

In January 1522 the Spanish ships left for home, sailing west. They were laden with spices and jewels. The *Trinidad,* Magellan's flagship, was captured by the Portuguese. But the *Vittoria,* leaking badly and crewed only by Elcano and eighteen survivors, limped home in September 1522 at the end of their epic around-the-world voyage.

Above *A modern painting of the Portuguese explorer, Ferdinand Magellan.*

Protestant pirates

Spain may have lost the spice trade but in the New World she found even more valuable merchandise — silver. By 1580 huge cargoes of silver were reaching Spain annually. The pope had given the New World to Catholic Spain but Protestant sailors from England, France and Holland ignored this. For them the Spanish galleons loaded with treasure were tempting targets.

Francis Drake (1540-96) had made his reputation and fortune by plundering Spanish America. In 1572 he had successfully ambushed a whole convoy in Panama. Now, in 1577, Queen Elizabeth I of England gave him secret instructions for a new venture. England and Spain were not at war, so Elizabeth had to be careful. Drake was probably asked to find the continent in the Pacific, Terra Australis, robbing Spanish ships and settlements on the way.

Above *A portrait of Elizabeth I, queen of England from 1558-1603.*

Like Magellan, Drake took five ships, although his were smaller. The *Christopher* was only fifteen tons! He sailed to South America, where he had to execute an old friend to quell a mutiny, and reached the Straits of Magellan with three ships in August 1578. One ship now sank in a terrible storm that lasted for fifty-two days, and the *Christopher* went home. Drake himself, in the *Golden Hind*, was blown into the open sea south of Chile.

Drake's fortune now turned. He sailed up the west coast of South America raiding Spanish ports and ships as he went. The *Golden Hind*, filled with treasure, at last headed for home across the Pacific in July 1579.

After further adventures, including being stranded on a reef, Drake reached Plymouth on November 3, 1580. A few days later Drake was knighted by his grateful queen on the deck of the *Golden Hind*.

Above *A painting of the English explorer, Francis Drake.*

Opposite *During his circumnavigation of the world from 1577-80, Drake captured the Spanish galleon* Spitfire *which was laden with riches.*

7 TO THE FROZEN NORTH

A northwest passage

Above *A painting of Martin Frobisher, an English sailor who made several unsuccessful expeditions to find a northwest passage to Asia.*

Sir Humphrey Gilbert had sensibly written in 1576 that a passage tp Asia ought to exist around the north of North America. The search for this channel was carried out almost entirely by Englishmen. What was not realized however, was the difficulty of navigating a northwest passage to Asia ought to exist around the north of North

The Yorkshireman Martin Frobisher led the first expedition of three small ships in 1576. He found no passage to Asia, but he brought home an eskimo and some fool's gold. The merchants of London believed that Frobisher had found gold and they funded two more expeditions. From the last trip Frobisher brought back 1,350 tons of worthless ore: his company collapsed.

The next man to look for the northwest passage was John Davis. During his three voyages, starting in 1585, his men were terribly bitten by "muskytoes" (the old-fashioned spelling of mosquitoes), while their ships risked being crushed by "islands of ice" (icebergs). But still no way to the East was found.

In 1610 the skilled and experienced explorer Henry Hudson tried to find a northwest passage. He and the crew of his ship, the *Discovery*, spent the winter in a huge bay, now known as Hudson Bay, convinced that this was the opening to the Pacific. But in the spring Hudson's men discovered that their leader had been stealing food from them, so he was set adrift to die in an open boat.

By 1616 Robert Bylot and William Baffin had shown Hudson Bay to be a dead end. They had also pushed up the Davis Strait as far as they could, before deciding that there was no practical route to Asia that way. Only in 1906 did a ship successfully navigate the treacherous northwest passage.

Below *Henry Hudson's expedition in 1610 failed to find a northwest passage to Asia. His disappointed crew mutinied and set him adrift to die in Hudson Bay.*

A northeast passage

It was not until 1553 that a serious attempt was made to discover a northeast passage around Norway to Asia. The expedition was led by Sir Hugh Willoughby and Richard Chancellor, but the two became separated in a storm off Norway. In 1554 Willoughby's two ships were caught in the ice and all the men froze to death.

Chancellor was more lucky. He founded a trading post at Archangel, then traveled south to Moscow where he met the Russian leader, Tsar Ivan the Terrible. As a result of this visit, the Muscovy Company was formed in London to trade with the Russians. But a northeast passage was no nearer discovery.

Below *In 1596 the Dutch explorer William Barents spent winter in the frozen wastes of Novaya Zemlya, on island in the Arctic Ocean.*

In 1556 and 1580 further expeditions set out. Both reached the Kara Sea, but were turned back by the "terrible abundance of ice" and the early arrival of winter.

The most famous explorer of these bleak waters was the Dutchman, William Barents. On his first voyage in 1594 he discovered Spitzbergen and Bear Island. Two years later Barents found the islands of Novaya Zemlya and he and his crew spent a long, frozen winter there in a little hut made of driftwood. The men survived by eating the meat of Polar bears and burning their fat in lamps. But the diet left the men open to scurvy, which killed Barents on the journey home in 1597.

Barents's hut was rediscovered in 1871 very much as it had been left. Eight years later the 300-ton steamship, *Vega*, finally sailed the northeast passage.

Above *Ivan the Terrible, tsar of Russia from 1547-84.*

8 SHIPS AND THE SEA

The ships

The voyages of Columbus and the other explorers were possible only because ship design had been much improved in the fifteenth century. Two different types of vessels had been successfully united.

In the Middle Ages the usual North European ship was the cog. These short, tubby boats had big cargo holds and square sails, set on a single mast supported by ratlines, or ladders of rope. The rudder was in the center of the stern, and the oak planks of the sides overlapped each other in a "clinker" construction. These tough little ships were very seaworthy, but clumsy and slow.

Mediterranean ships were quite different. They were built around a long oak frame, with planks placed edge to edge in what is called "carvel" construction. They were usually steered by a large oar at the stern, and they had lateen (triangular) sails. Such vessels were sleek, fast and maneuverable, but unstable in rough seas.

By 1450 these two designs had come together to produce the incredibly tough ships used by the explorers. They had carvel sides, nailed to long frames, but with raised bows and sterns to keep large waves from swamping them. The cog's stern rudder was used. They often had three masts with ratlines, on which square sails could be mixed with lateen. Columbus's *Pinta* changed from lateen to square rig in the Caribbean. The bigger ships, up to 1,000 tons, were called carracks; the smaller ones, like those used by Diaz, were caravels.

The explorers' ships were seldom the best available. One man looking at Magellan's fleet in harbor thought that it was too rotten to put to sea! No one risked their most valuable vessels on voyages from which there was a good chance that they would never return.

Above *This man is working to improve the design of ships to make them more seaworthy.*

Below *Ship design improved a great deal during the Age of Exploration. Once built, ships had to be well-stocked with provisions for the long voyages ahead.*

35

The sea

At about 40° south, gale force winds, known as the "Roaring Forties," blow continually from west to east. They howl round Cape Horn, at the tip of South America, raising waves of 15 meters (50 feet) — as tall as Magellan's caravel, the *Santiago*. Even today, sailing vessels enter this area with reluctance. Imagine the problems faced by Drake and Magellan, meeting these seas for the first time.

Westerly winds blow in the northern hemisphere, too, at about 40°. It was these winds that brought Columbus swiftly home from the Caribbean. The Gulf Stream — a strong, warm ocean current — also helped him to Europe.

Below *The map shows the routes taken by Ferdinand Magellan, Francis Drake and James Cook on their epic voyages around the world, and Columbus's voyage to the West Indies in 1492.*

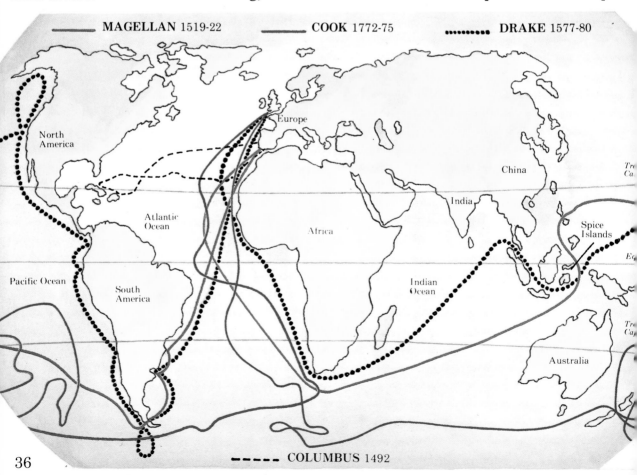

MAGELLAN 1519-22   COOK 1772-75   •••••••• DRAKE 1577-80

- - - - - COLUMBUS 1492

Left *A ship under sail, drawn by the German painter, Hans Holbein, in 1532.*

Near the Equator the winds are more variable. To the north they tend to blow from the east toward the Equator. This explains why Columbus reached the West Indies and not the area of Washington, which is on the same latitude as Spain. Vasco da Gama, however, was fortunate in finding a pilot who took him across the Indian Ocean during the southwest monsoon. The voyage took him a month. He chose the wrong time of year to return, however, and took four months to cross to Africa.

In the southern hemisphere the prevailing (usual) winds blow from the southwest toward the Equator. These carried Drake rapidly up the coast of South America, but caused the Portuguese problems off southwest Africa. On the Equator and around the Tropics of Cancer and Capricorn the winds are unpredictable, which made Magellan's crossing of the Pacific so difficult.

The directions of the winds and currents, the mighty waves, the calms and the ice are all essential knowledge for modern sailors. The men of Columbus's day, hardly used to sailing out of the sight of land, knew almost nothing of them. They learned the hard way — through experience.

Navigation

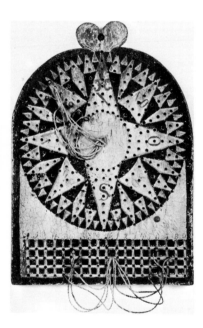

Above *Davis's quadrant, a navigational aid in use by 1600.*

Medieval mariners found their way by keeping within sight of land. This was called pilotage. Navigation, which means finding a course across the open sea, was hardly needed until Columbus's time, and not until 1581 did a book on seamanship first make clear the difference between pilotage and navigation.

A captain's traditional aids were the lookout, usually at the top of the mast; the lead, which was lowered over the side to measure the depth; and the log. This was a piece of wood, attached to a knotted rope. When it was thrown over the side it floated and pulled out the rope: speed was then measured in knots. These remain the unit of speed for ships today. The log, unfortunately, did not allow for currents, so tides were always a problem when measuring speed, especially in unknown waters. Compasses were used, but magnetic variation was little understood.

Other instruments found a ship's latitude, or distance from the Equator, by measuring the height above the horizon of the sun or a prominent star. At first a staff was used to help them in this task, but by the sixteenth century sailors were employing complicated backstaffs, astrolabes or quadrants, which did the job more efficiently. Davis's quadrant, which was the most accurate, was in use by 1600. These instruments meant that a sixteenth century sailor had a fair idea of his course.

There remained one real problem for navigators — longitude, or the measurement of distance to the east or west of a point. This can only be done with a chronometer, and these were not available for ships until the eighteenth century. Columbus and his contemporaries, therefore, were never able to fix their positions accurately, or the position of lands they discovered. So navigation remained a mixture of skill, experience — and luck.

Above *A traverse board, complete with string and pegs, used to plot a course.*

Opposite *The ship's log is thrown overboard to measure speed in knots.*

Preparing for a voyage

Before an explorer could start planning his expedition he needed a patron to provide the money. The early voyages of Diaz, Columbus or Cabot, were backed by royalty. Later, however, businessmen were prepared to risk their money. Hudson and Barents were supported in this way.

Once suitable ships were found, they had to be made ready. Most important was careening the ship's bottom, which meant scraping off all the barnacles and seaweed which had accumulated there. If this was not done, a ship's speed could be halved. On long voyages it had to be done en route, too. If there was enough money, all rotten wood had to be replaced, the sails and masts renewed, and plenty of spare ones made.

Above *An early mariner's compass,* c 1570.

Next the ships were loaded with every conceivable provision. Perishable food had to be salted or spiced to preserve it, and there were always plenty of dull but filling ship's biscuits. Drinking water was a problem because it soon became slimy and foul, so captains took plenty of wine and spirits, which did not go bad, to help keep the crew content. Navigational instruments, of course, were essential: Frobisher took twenty different kinds of compasses! Davis's men took coal to keep themselves warm in the Arctic, while on Columbus's second voyage he took farm animals and everything necessary to found a colony.

Weapons were always taken. The ships carried cannon and for the men there were swords, pikes, muskets and armor. Most expeditions also carried articles of trade such as knives, bells, fish hooks, bracelets, mirrors and beads. Catholic explorers usually sought the pope's approval, and Diaz spent the night before he left in silent prayer. No matter how careful the preparations, all sailors knew that their fate would not be entirely in their own hands.

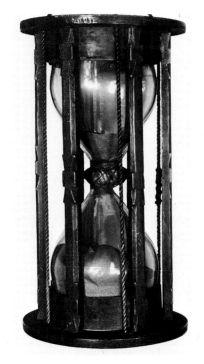

Above A sand-glass used to time the watches — the division of the nautical day into four-hour periods.

Below There was nothing glamorous about a long voyage in a wooden ship, so some of the crew had been bullied into joining up.

9 SAILORS

A ship's crew

Above *An English ship's master at the time of the Spanish Armada in 1588.*

Opposite *Chasing this monkey up the rigging was one of the rare moments of fun enjoyed by the ship's boy.*

Columbus's crews are the first in the Age of Exploration about whom we have accurate information. Apart from the Italian captain, there were Spaniards, Portuguese, Frenchmen, Germans and Dutchmen. Magellan's men were even more varied, and included Greeks, a gunner from Bristol and Magellan's personal negro slave. Crews were employed very casually. The word went round the taverns and fishing villages that an expedition was forming and men came forward to sign on. Most would be experienced sailors, but each voyage attracted debtors, criminals and other undesirable characters whom people wanted to get rid of. Women remained at home.

The majority of the crew were ordinary seamen, expected to lend a hand at any task from lookout to hoisting a sail. There were also skilled tradesmen, like carpenters, sailmakers, surgeons and cooks — who had a tricky time cooking food on an open fire in a wooden ship. The caulker was responsible for keeping the ship's seams watertight; the cooper had the vital job of looking after all barrels, in which food and water were stored. John Davis was unusual in taking musicians on one of his voyages. All men had to be versatile. A carpenter, for example, might have to make a new rudder in mid-ocean.

Most important were the master (or captain), his mate, the boatswain, pilot and steward. The mate was the captain's deputy and helped the pilot with navigation. The boatswain (or bosun) was in charge of all the ship's gear: sails, ropes, anchors and so forth; the steward was responsible for food and stores, and for the ship's boys. These were young lads who led tough lives carrying out numerous little tasks about the ship.

Life on board

Life on board a sixteenth century ship was very uncomfortable. Drake's *Golden Hind* was only 30 meters (100 feet) long but a crew of eighty was crammed into her. In Columbus's day the men slept on deck in fine weather, or on the ballast when it was stormy. Sand ballast was comfortable, but it soaked up water and sewage as the voyage progressed. Later it became more usual for the men to sleep on hammocks in the forecastle (the raised area at the bow). Most crews were divided into two watches, which took it in turns to do four-hour spells of duty.

Once at sea there was little opportunity for men to wash. There were no toilets on board either; just a box hung over the side. Even this was too dangerous to use in rough weather. The only fresh food was fish. The normal diet was an unhealthy routine of salt meat, biscuit and cheese, washed down with an average of one-and-a-half liters of wine each per day. In these cramped, unhealthy

conditions, with broken sleep, and fed on terrible food, men were expected to work unceasingly.

Since wooden ships leaked continually, the pumps had to be manned daily. The sails were in constant need of adjustment. Ropes had to be replaced and repaired, the decks had to be washed, anchors raised or lowered, and on larger ships it took ten men just to hold the tiller! In an emergency the sailors would even be expected to fight. So, by day and night, a vessel at sea was an overcrowded hive of endless, dangerous activity.

Below *Living conditions on board a ship at sea were cramped and uncomfortable. When not working, there was little to do besides eat, drink and sleep.*

Death on board

"All their skin was spotted with marks of blood of a purple color. Their mouths became stinking, their gums rotten so that all the flesh did fall out." This was scurvy, the disease which killed far more sailors in the Age of Exploration than anything else. Within six weeks all but ten of Cartier's men had died and it killed thirty of da Gama's men as they returned across the Indian Ocean. We now know that scurvy is caused by a lack of fresh fruit and vegetables in the diet. Later captains prevented it by carrying hundreds of oranges and lemons, but for the men of Magellan's time scurvy remained a mystery — and a killer.

Above *In 1535 Jacques Cartier, a Frenchman, explored the St Lawrence River in what is now Canada. Many of his crew died of scurvy.*

Besides scurvy, the sailors on long voyages suffered from many other terrible diseases. The cramped, airless conditions below decks bred pneumonia and tuberculosis, while the lack of proper sanitation gave rise to dysentery, typhoid and food poisoning. To make matters worse, in the tropics they came across malaria and yellow fever for the first time.

The accident rate, too, was very high on board ship. The whiplash of breaking cables could slice off an arm or leg. Frequently sailors fell from the rigging on to the deck or into the sea. Men in the crow's nest could be struck by lightning, while down below decks they were continually hitting their heads on the low beams.

As if all this was not enough, there were the perils of shipwreck, fire, cold or armed clash with an enemy. Very few sailors reached old age and many of those who did were badly disfigured or disabled.

Opposite *Working on board ship was a dangerous occupation and there were often fatal accidents when men fell from the rigging.*

Mutiny

The ordinary sailors of the Age of Exploration wanted to get rich quickly. For this they would risk their lives, and there was always a chance that they might strike it lucky. Drake's voyage round the world made a huge profit and the survivors all received their share. But when danger lurked and the chances of wealth seemed slight, the men would grumble.

Mutiny was always just below the surface on the voyages of exploration. The crews were hard, ignorant men, who could neither read nor write: some really feared that Columbus was leading them off the edge of the world when they sailed for so long in 1492. The captain used a

skillful mixture of force and persuasion to urge them to carry on, but there was still trouble. How did the rudder of the *Pinta* break off? Accident or sabotage?

The leaders of expeditions had to be ruthless in dealing with mutiny. At Port St. Julian, now in Argentina, Magellan heard whispers of rebellion among his captains. Men were executed, and a captain was marooned. Fifty-seven years later, in exactly the same place, Francis Drake heard similar dangerous talk. He beheaded the ringleader, his friend Thomas Doughty, while the skulls of Magellan's victims, still on the beach, looked grimly on.

Henry Hudson made the mistake of angering his crew and paid the price. He was cast adrift in an open boat by his mutinous crew and was never heard of again.

Below *In Port St Julian in South America, Drake ordered the execution of the mutineer, Doughty. The skulls were of men who had mutinied on Magellan's voyage, 57 years earlier.*

49

10 ONE WORLD

Later voyages

The urge to explore did not stop as the Age of Exploration drew to a close at the end of the sixteenth century. A whole continent, Australasia, had yet to be discovered, and no one had conquered the northwest or northeast passages. But most of the great discoveries for Europeans were now inland, as explorers pushed into America, Africa, Arabia and other unmapped areas of the globe.

The last great unexplored ocean was the Pacific. From the sixteenth century Spanish galleons carried silver from Acapulco in Mexico to Manila in the Philippine Islands, returning with cargoes of silk. The Dutch had sailed to western Australia in the early seventeenth century, but it was not until the time of Captain James Cook (1728-79) that the true geography of the Pacific became known. Beginning in 1768, Cook made three voyages exploring eastern Australia, New Zealand, New Guinea and the Bering Strait between Russia and Alaska. However, he was tragically killed in Hawaii, trying to prevent his men from firing on the inhabitants of the islands.

By about the middle of the twentieth century every corner of the planet had been visited. Explorers had charted the oceans and mapped the continents, visited both poles, plumbed the depths of the seas and climbed the highest peaks. But the quest for new frontiers had not dimmed. In 1957 the Russians put a satellite into orbit round the earth. Four years later Yuri Gagarin became the first person in space, and in 1969 Neil Armstrong set foot on the moon. Perhaps another Age of Exploration has only just begun.

Above *Captain James Cook, whose voyages of exploration in the eighteenth century were very important in opening up the Pacific Ocean.*

Opposite *In 1770 Captain Cook's ship, the* Endeavour, *ran aground on the Great Barrier Reef off the east coast of Australia.*

51

The price of discovery

In many ways the voyages of discovery were just the introduction to a much longer story. After the great navigators came the soldiers, merchants, missionaries and settlers. In some parts of the world, India for example, Europeans were content at first just to set up trading posts. But in others, like Mexico, Australia or North America, they were satisfied with nothing less than taking over the newly discovered lands for themselves. Thus it was that in the wake of the explorers came three evils: disease, slavery and empire.

Smallpox and typhoid were the two killer diseases which the Spaniards carried to the New World. The devastation they produced was horrifying: three-and-a-half million people died in Mexico's first smallpox epidemic. Between 1519 and 1597 the population of cen-

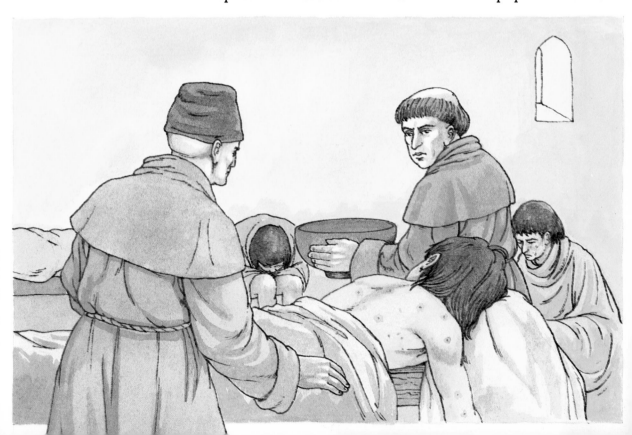

tral Mexico fell from eleven million to just over two million.

When the Europeans first arrived in Africa they found a slave trade already in existence, run largely by Arabs. In European hands the terrible trade grew and hundreds of thousands of Africans were shipped to the under-populated mainland or Caribbean islands in the New World. In the sixteenth century 16,000 slaves a year left West Africa for Spanish and Portuguese territories there.

The Europeans were technologically advanced, especially in the manufacture of weapons of war. With cannon and musket they forced their way into the spice trade, while in the New World the Portuguese, Spanish, French, Dutch and English conquered vast colonies for themselves. They peopled these overseas territories with emigrants from Europe, and the native "Indians" were enslaved, slaughtered or reduced to second-class citizens. The original inhabitants of the troubled lands must have wished the explorers had never set sail.

Below *Disease and slavery followed in the wake of the European explorers. Native populations were often enslaved or struck down by diseases like smallpox.*

A shrinking world

Above *The illustration above shows four of the greatest sailors of the Age of Exploration: from left to right, Columbus, Magellan, Drake and Cook. Columbus's hand rests on an astrolabe, a navigational aid used to measure the height of the stars. The ship is the* Golden Hind, *Drake's flagship.*

The Age of Exploration marked the beginning of a very important new period in world history. Previously the great civilizations of China, India, Europe and the Americas existed independently of each other. Europe itself was inward-looking and defensive. By 1800 this had changed. There was regular contact between all the major regions of the world, and almost everywhere the European way of life was threatening to dominate. The balance of world power had altered dramatically.

The great voyages of exploration brought together people of different countries, races and religions. Christianity was carried to all corners of the globe, while Europeans were made aware of other religions for the first time. Animals and plants were carried by the soldiers and merchants. Sheep and horses were brought to the New World by the Spanish. Potatoes, previously found only in the New World, flourished in Europe. Wheat and sugar cane spread from the East Indies to suitable climates round the world. Even racial groups were intermingled as Europeans emigrated and Africans were ruthlessly transported from one continent to another.

These developments were slow but significant. What emerged from them was the world as we know it today, where no nation or culture exists in isolation from any other. Never in their wildest dreams can those brave captains and their crews have imagined what they were starting, as long ago they hoisted their sails and set forth to explore new lands.

Table of dates

1000? Vikings discover Vinland (North America).

1271 Marco Polo sets out for China.

1432 Portuguese discover the Azores Islands.

1437 Henry the Navigator founds his base at Sagres.

1455 Gambia discovered.

1484 Portuguese reach the mouth of the Congo.

1487 Covilhao sets out to journey overland to Asia.
Diaz's expedition leaves for the Cape of Storms.

1492-93 Columbus's first voyage, to the West Indies.

1497 Cabot discovers Newfoundland.

1497-99 da Gama sails to India and back.

1498 Columbus's third voyage, to Venezuela.

1499 Vespucci discovers Guiana.

1500 Cabral discovers Brazil.

1502-04 Columbus's final voyage, to Nicaragua.

1511 Portuguese ships reach the Spice Islands in the East Indies.

1516 Portuguese sailors visit China.

1519-22 Magellan/Elcano sail round the world.

1519 Pineda explores the Gulf of Mexico.

1524 Verrazano explores the coast of North America.

1534-35 Cartier explores the St. Lawrence River in Canada.

1553 Willoughby and Chancellor look for the northeast passage.

1576 Frobisher sails to look for the northwest passage.

1577-80 Drake sails around the world.

1581 Davis's first voyage in search of a northeast passage.

1594 Barents joins the search for a northeast passage.

1602 Jantszoon reaches Australia.

1611 Hudson cast adrift and dies in the bay now called Hudson's Bay.

1642 Tasman discovers New Zealand.

1768-71 Cook sails around the world and starts his exploration of the Pacific.

1772-75 Cook's second expedition to the Pacific.

New words

Ballast The weight at the bottom of a ship that helps it to float upright.

Chart A map of a sea or coast used by sailors.

Chronometer An accurate clock that is not affected by movement.

Colony An overseas possession of a country.

Compass A magnetic instrument for finding direction. A compass needle always points north.

Convoy A number of ships or vehicles traveling together for safety.

Crow's Nest A platform at the top of a mast.

Delta A fan-shaped formation created when a river divides into several channels just before it reaches the sea.

Emigrant A person who leaves the land of his birth and settles in another country.

Empire Lands in different parts of the world ruled by one powerful country.

Equator An imaginary line around the center of the earth.

Fool's Gold Pyrite, a worthless yellow mineral that looks like gold.

Galleon A large sailing ship with three masts that developed from the carrack.

Hemisphere Half of the world divided into north and south.

Infidel "Unbeliever." Used by Christians to refer to people of other religious beliefs.

Knight A title given to someone as a reward. Knights are allowed to call themselves "Sir"; for example Sir Francis Drake.

Magnetic Variation Error in a compass caused by unusual magnetic rocks in the earth.

Medieval Anything connected with the "Middle Ages," approximately AD 1000 to AD 1500.

Missonary A person who tries to spread his or her religious faith to other countries.

Patron A person who supports a project, such as a voyage of discovery, with money or other help.

Peninsula Land jutting into the sea and surrounded by water on three sides.

Protestants Christians, led by Martin Luther, who broke away from the Roman Catholic Church in the sixteenth century.

Rigging Ropes supporting masts and sails.

Rudder A large flat board at the stern of a ship used for steering.

Spices Strongly flavored vegetable substances used in cooking, and for preserving food: for example pepper and cloves.

Strait A narrow channel of sea between two areas of land.

Tiller A long lever of wood by which the rudder is moved to left or right.

Tropic Two imaginary lines running round the world at 23½ degrees. The northern one is the Tropic of Cancer, the southern one the Tropic of Capricorn.

Tsar The title once used by emperors of Russia.

Further information

Fritz, Jean. *Where Do You Think You're Going, Christopher Columbus?* New York: Putnam, 1980.

Goodnough, David. *Francis Drake.* Mahwah, NJ: Troll Associates, 1979.

————. *John Cabot and Son.* Mahwah, NJ: Troll Associates, 1979.

Grosseck, Joyce. *Great Explorers,* revised edition. Grand Rapids, MI: Fideler, 1981.

Harley, Ruth. *Henry Hudson.* Mahwah, NJ: Troll Associates, 1979.

Hoobler, Dorothy and Hoobler, Thomas. *The Voyages of Captain Cook.* New York: Putnam, 1983.

Johnson, Spencer. *The Value of Curiosity: The Story of Christopher Columbus.* San Diego, CA: Value Communications/Oak Tree Publications, 1977.

Knight, David. *Vasco da Gama.* Mahwah, NJ: Troll Associates, 1979.

Langdon-Davies, John. *Columbus and the Discovery of America.* New York: Viking, 1972.

Levy, Elizabeth. *Marco Polo.* New York: Random, 1982.

McCall, Edith. *Explorers in a New World.* Chicago, IL: Childrens Press, 1980.

Reeves, Marjorie. *Explorers of the Elizabethan Age.* New York: Longman, 1977.

Sandak, Cass R. *Explorers and Discovery.* New York: Franklin Watts, 1983.

Townson, W.D. *Illustrated Atlas of the World in the Age of Discovery.* New York: Warwick Press/Franklin Watts, 1981.

Wilkie, Katherine. *Ferdinand Magellan: Noble Captain.* Boston, MA: Houghton Mifflin, 1963.

Index

Picture acknowledgments

The illustrations in this book were supplied by: Mansell Collection 17, 23, 33, 46; Malcolm S. Walker 27.
The remainder are from the Wayland Picture Library.